# The Pebble® First Guide to the Solar System

## by Joanne Mattern

**Consulting Editor:** Gail Saunders-Smith, PhD

**Consultant:** Stephen J. Kortenkamp, PhD
Senior Scientist
Planetary Science Institute
Tucson, Arizona

Capstone
press®

Mankato, Minnesota

Pebble Books are published by Capstone Press,
151 Good Counsel Drive, P.O. Box 669, Mankato, Minnesota 56002.
www.capstonepress.com

Books published by Capstone Press are manufactured with paper
containing at least 10 percent post-consumer waste.

*Library of Congress Cataloging-in-Publication Data*
Mattern, Joanne, 1963–
    The Pebble first guide to the solar system / by Joanne Mattern.
    p. cm. — (Pebble books. Pebble first guides)
    Summary: "A basic field guide format introduces the planets, dwarf
planets, the Sun, and the Moon. Includes color photographs and solar system
illustrations" — Provided by publisher.
    Includes bibliographical references and index.
    ISBN: 978-1-4296-3300-0 (library binding)
    ISBN: 978-1-4296-3864-7 (paperback)
    1. Solar system — Juvenile literature. I. Title. II. Series.
QB501.3.M38 2010
523.2 — dc22                                                2009004923

## About the Solar System

The solar system has much to discover. This book features the
Sun, Earth's moon, the eight planets, and five dwarf planets. The
measurements given in this book are rounded to the nearest digit.

## Note to Parents and Teachers

The Pebble First Guides set supports science standards related to
earth science. This book describes and illustrates the solar system.
This book introduces early readers to subject-specific vocabulary
words, which are defined in the Glossary section. Early readers may
need assistance to read some words and to use the Table of Contents,
Glossary, Read More, Internet Sites, and Index sections of the book.

# Table of Contents

# Sun

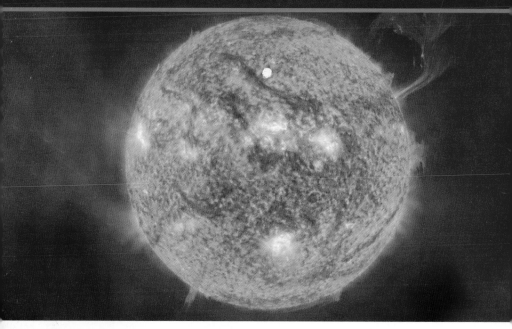

| | |
|---|---|
| **Distance from Earth:** | about 93 million miles (150 million kilometers) |
| **Diameter:** | 870,000 miles (1.4 million kilometers) |
| **Temperature (surface):** | 10,000 degrees Fahrenheit (5,500 degrees Celsius) |
| **Facts:** | • center of the solar system<br>• closest star to Earth |

surface of Sun

Milky Way

Sun

5

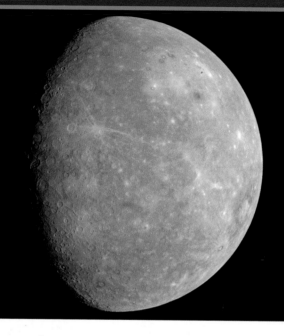

| | |
|---|---|
| **Distance from Sun:** | about 36 million miles (58 million kilometers) |
| **Diameter:** | about 3,000 miles (5,000 kilometers) |
| **Temperature (surface):** | −270 to +800 degrees Fahrenheit (−170 to +425 degrees Celsius) |
| **Facts:** | • smallest planet in the solar system<br>• closest planet to the Sun |

Sun

Mercury

Venus

Earth

Moon

Mars

Asteroid Belt

Saturn

Jupiter

Ceres
(dwarf planet)

Uranus

Neptune

Eris
(dwarf planet)

Pluto
(dwarf planet)

Makemake
(dwarf planet)

Haumea
(dwarf planet)

surface of Mercury

| | |
|---|---|
| **Distance from Sun:** | 67 million miles (108 million kilometers) |
| **Diameter:** | 7,500 miles (12,100 kilometers) |
| **Temperature (surface):** | about 900 degrees Fahrenheit (480 degrees Celsius) |
| **Facts:** | • hottest planet surface<br>• brightest planet seen from Earth |

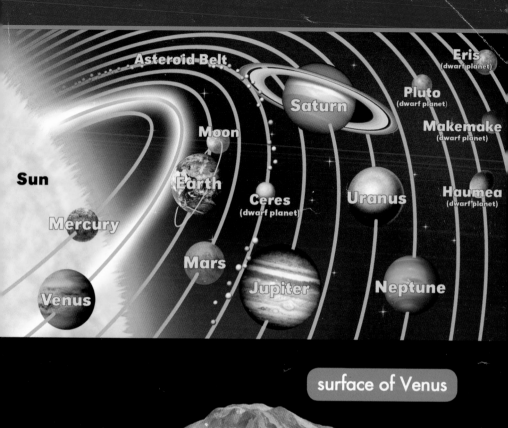

Asteroid Belt

Saturn

Moon

Eris
(dwarf planet)

Pluto
(dwarf planet)

Makemake
(dwarf planet)

Sun

Earth

Ceres
(dwarf planet)

Uranus

Haumea
(dwarf planet)

Mercury

Mars

Jupiter

Neptune

Venus

surface of Venus

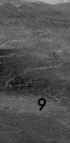

| | |
|---|---|
| **Distance from Sun:** | 93 million miles (150 million kilometers) |
| **Diameter:** | about 7,900 miles (12,700 kilometers) |
| **Temperature (surface):** | −130 to +140 degrees Fahrenheit (−90 to +60 degrees Celsius) |
| **Facts:** | • only planet with oceans on the surface<br>• only planet known to support life |

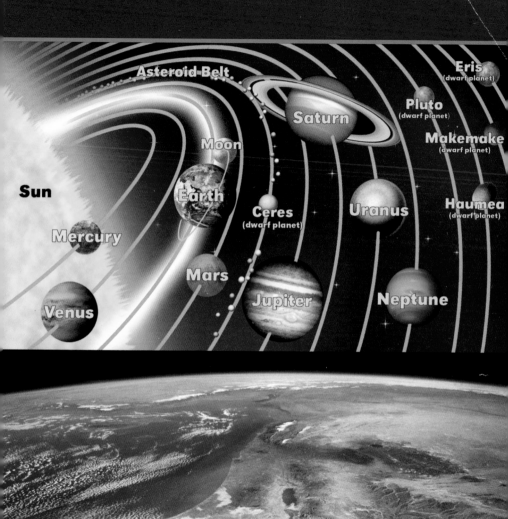

Asteroid Belt

Eris
(dwarf planet)

Pluto
(dwarf planet)

Saturn

Makemake
(dwarf planet)

Moon

Sun

Earth

Ceres
(dwarf planet)

Uranus

Haumea
(dwarf planet)

Mercury

Mars

Venus

Jupiter

Neptune

surface of Earth

# Moon

| | |
|---|---|
| **Distance from Earth:** | about 239,000 miles (385,000 kilometers) |
| **Diameter:** | about 2,160 miles (3,500 kilometers) |
| **Temperature (surface):** | −290 to +266 degrees Fahrenheit (−180 to +130 degrees Celsius) |
| **Facts:** | • Earth's natural satellite<br>• gray dust and rocks cover surface |

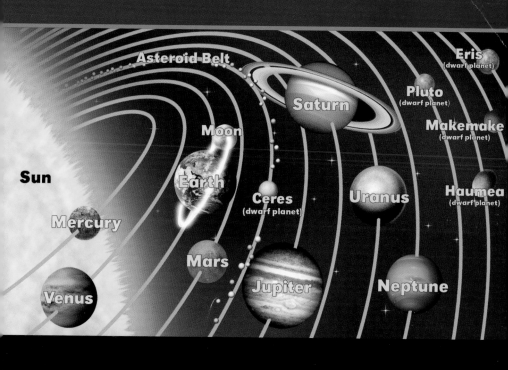

Sun

Mercury

Venus

Asteroid Belt

Moon

Earth

Mars

Ceres
(dwarf planet)

Saturn

Jupiter

Uranus

Neptune

Eris
(dwarf planet)

Pluto
(dwarf planet)

Makemake
(dwarf planet)

Haumea
(dwarf planet)

surface of Moon

| Distance from Sun: | about 142 million miles (228 million kilometers) |
| --- | --- |
| Diameter: | about 4,200 miles (6,800 kilometers) |
| Temperature (surface): | −220 to +70 degrees Fahrenheit (−140 to +20 degrees Celsius) |
| Facts: | • called the Red Planet<br>• strong winds cause giant dust storms |

14

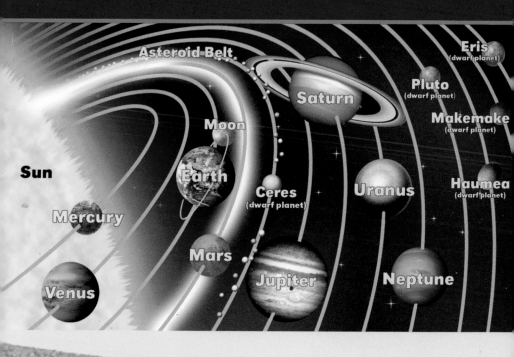

Sun

Mercury

Venus

Asteroid Belt

Moon

Earth

Mars

Saturn

Ceres
(dwarf planet)

Jupiter

Uranus

Neptune

Eris
(dwarf planet)

Pluto
(dwarf planet)

Makemake
(dwarf planet)

Haumea
(dwarf planet)

surface of Mars

15

| | |
|---|---|
| **Distance from Sun:** | about 480 million miles (770 million kilometers) |
| **Diameter:** | about 89,000 miles (143,000 kilometers) |
| **Temperature (cloud top):** | −162 degrees Fahrenheit (−108 degrees Celsius) |

**Facts:**
- largest planet in the solar system
- volcanoes on moon Io erupt into space

16

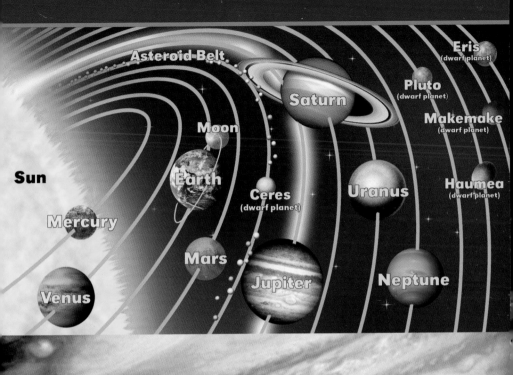

Sun

Mercury

Venus

Asteroid Belt

Moon

Earth

Mars

Ceres
(dwarf planet)

Jupiter

Saturn

Uranus

Neptune

Eris
(dwarf planet)

Pluto
(dwarf planet)

Makemake
(dwarf planet)

Haumea
(dwarf planet)

Io

| | |
|---|---|
| **Distance from Sun:** | about 890 million miles (1.4 billion kilometers) |
| **Diameter:** | about 75,000 miles (120,000 kilometers) |
| **Temperature (cloud top):** | −285 degrees Fahrenheit (−176 degrees Celsius) |
| **Facts:** | • rings made of ice circle planet<br>• has 60 known satellites |

Sun

Mercury

Venus

Asteroid Belt

Moon

Earth

Mars

Saturn

Ceres
(dwarf planet)

Jupiter

Uranus

Neptune

Eris
(dwarf planet)

Pluto
(dwarf planet)

Makemake
(dwarf planet)

Haumea
(dwarf planet)

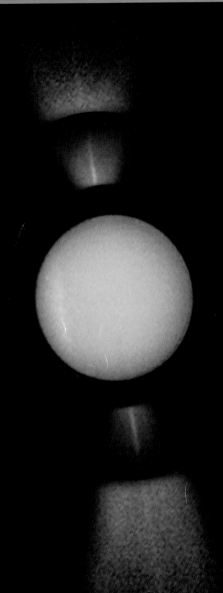

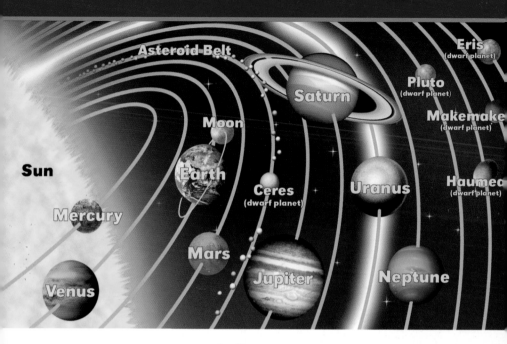

| Distance from Sun: | 1.7 billion miles (2.7 billion kilometers) |
| Diameter: | about 32,000 miles (51,500 kilometers) |
| Temperature (cloud top): | −355 degrees Fahrenheit (−215 degrees Celsius) |
| Facts: | • first planet discovered with a telescope<br>• spins on its side |

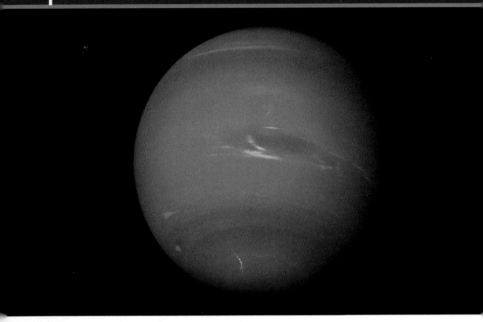

| | |
|---|---|
| **Distance from Sun:** | 2.8 billion miles (4.5 billion kilometers) |
| **Diameter:** | about 31,000 miles (49,900 kilometers) |
| **Temperature (cloud top):** | −353 degrees Fahrenheit (−214 degrees Celsius) |
| **Facts:** | • farthest planet from the Sun<br>• white clouds move across planet |

Asteroid Belt

Eris
(dwarf planet)

Pluto
(dwarf planet)

Saturn

Makemake
(dwarf planet)

Moon

Earth

Ceres
(dwarf planet)

Uranus

Haume
(dwarf planet)

Sun

Mercury

Mars

Jupiter

Neptune

Venus

clouds

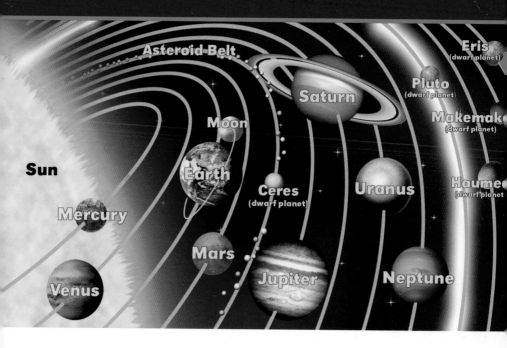

| | |
|---|---|
| **Distance from Sun:** | 3 billion miles (4.8 billion kilometers) |
| **Diameter:** | about 1,400 miles (2,250 kilometers) |
| **Temperature (surface):** | −382 degrees Fahrenheit (−230 degrees Celsius) |
| **Facts:** | • classified as a dwarf planet in 2006 <br> • smaller than Earth's moon |

25

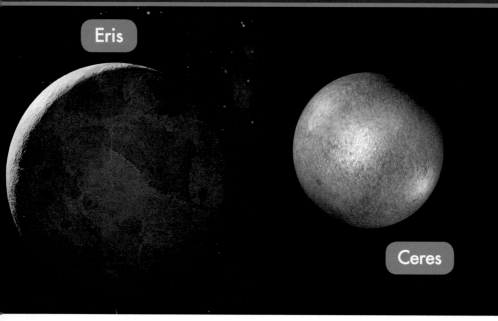

Eris

Ceres

| | |
|---|---|
| **Distance from Sun:** | about 9 billion miles (14 billion kilometers) |
| **Diameter:** | about 1,800 miles (2,900 kilometers) |
| **Temperature (surface):** | −470 degrees Fahrenheit (−279 degrees Celsius) |
| **Facts:** | • largest dwarf planet • farthest known object orbiting the Sun |

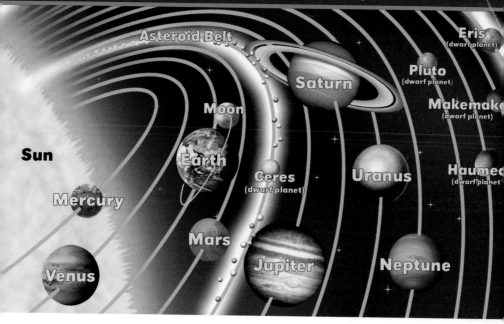

| | |
|---|---|
| **Distance from Sun:** | about 240 million miles (380 million kilometers) |
| **Diameter:** | about 600 miles (950 kilometers) |
| **Temperature (surface):** | −160 degrees Fahrenheit (−110 degrees Celsius) |
| **Facts:** | • only dwarf planet in the asteroid belt <br> • once classified as a planet |

27

# Makemake

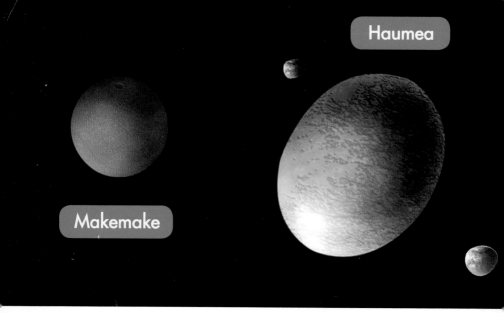

Haumea

Makemake

| | |
|---|---|
| **Distance from Sun:** | 4.8 billion miles (7.7 billion kilometers) |
| **Diameter:** | about 900 miles (1,500 kilometers) |
| **Temperature (surface):** | −400 degrees Fahrenheit (−240 degrees Celsius) |
| **Facts:** | • classified as a dwarf planet in 2008<br>• reddish in color |

28

# Haumea

**Say It: HAH-oo-may**

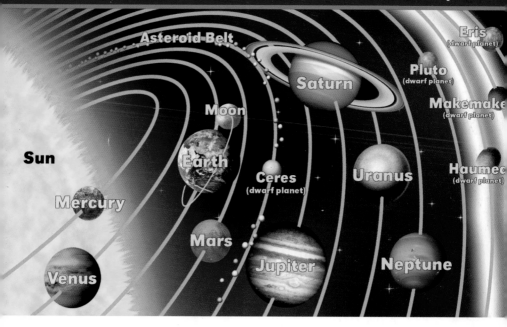

| | |
|---|---|
| **Distance from Sun:** | 4.7 billion miles (7.6 billion kilometers) |
| **Diameter:** | about 600 to 1,200 miles (950 to 1,900 kilometers) |
| **Temperature (surface):** | −400 degrees Fahrenheit (−240 degrees Celsius) |
| **Facts:** | • fifth dwarf planet; named in 2008<br>• shaped like a football |

# Glossary

asteroid belt — the area in space between Mars and Jupiter where the most asteroids are found

classified — put into a group

cloud top — the highest point of a cloud layer

dwarf planet — a rounded object that moves around the Sun, but is too small to be a planet

erupt — to suddenly burst

orbit — the path an object follows as it goes around the Sun or a planet

satellite — a moon or other object that travels around another object in space

surface — the outside or outermost area of something

temperature — the measure of how hot or cold something is

# Read More

**Bredeson, Carmen**. *What Is the Solar System?* I Like Space! Berkeley Heights, N.J.: Enslow, 2008.

**Rustad, Martha E. H.** *The Planets.* Out in Space. Mankato, Minn.: Capstone Press, 2009.

# Internet Sites

FactHound offers a safe, fun way to find Internet sites related to this book. All of the sites on FactHound have been researched by our staff.

Here's all you do:

Visit *www.facthound.com*

FactHound will fetch the best sites for you!

# Index

Grade: 1
Early-Intervention Level: 25

**Editorial Credits**
Katy Kudela, editor; Bobbi J. Wyss, book designer and illustrator;
   Alison Thiele, set designer; Jo Miller, media researcher


**Photo Credits**
JPL, 12; NASA, 5 (top), 11, 14, 15, 17, 19, 22, 24; NASA and The Hubble Heritage
Team (STScl/AURA), 18; NASA/ESA/A. Feild (for STScl), cover (Makemake),
28 (both); NASA/ESA/A. Schaller (for STScl), 26 (left); NASA/ESA/and M. Showalter
(SETI Institute), 20; NASA/Johns Hopkins University Applied Physics Laboratory/
Carnegie Institute of Washington, 6, 7; NASA/JPL, cover (montage of planets), cover
(Neptune), 9, 23; NASA/JPL-Caltech, 5 (bottom); NASA/JPL/Space Science Institute,
16; NASA/JPL/USGS, 13; NASA/JSC, cover (Earth); NASA/SOHO/EIT consortium,
4; NOAA/NASA GOES Project, 10; Photodisc, 8; Photo Researchers, Inc/Friedrich
Saurer, 26 (right)